FERN ANGI

The Art of Sh

C000301483

BROKEN SLEEP BOOKS

Published 2020,
Broken Sleep Books:
Cornwall / Wales

brokensleepbooks.com

Paperback Edition

Lay out your unrest.

Publisher/Editor: Aaron Kent
Editor: Charlie Baylis

Typeset in UK by Aaron Kent

Broken Sleep Books is committed to
a sustainable future for our planet,
and therefore uses print on
demand publication.

brokensleepbooks@gmail.com

ISBN: 978-1-913642-11-2

Contents

Words I learned to leave unsaid
for the women held in silent crypts inside me.

The Art of Shutting Up

Fern Angel Beattie

Preface

Woman

I am nothing without Woman. Of course, none of us are - literally - but if you've read either of my previous books you'll already be privy to the importance of women in my world; otherwise, anyone who knows me will tell you. *Senza una donna*, life is nix. Seriously, what's the point of it, if not to be curled up next to one? Even the act of dragging myself from my sleep each morning–that itself would be intolerable if not for the possibility of my dreams realised in flesh & bone. My feet swing over the side of the bed each morning and hit the ground without exception to the drum of Venus' pulse; a different rhythm for every dawn. Well, I have yet to love a Dawn, so in my case, for every Audrey, Natalie, Devon... the list is endless. Timeless. But you get the point.

My longing to both devour and emulate the best in women is intrinsic and deep-rooted. To extract, you would have to rip it from me like a pearl from the belly of an oyster and I would be left exposed: twitching and empty. Nowadays, women are saturated with discourse on the importance of loving themselves fiercely; having historically been less likely to do so without cloaking that love in an awkward cloud of apology, and, of course, I too am a woman and should worship myself as such. But you would think I was man – alien – by the ways in which I can be left astounded by my own gender time and again. It is women who fill me up. Each one I love her own ripe, fledgling universe, and I spend my life in a consistent state of flux, torn between a desire either to observe this universe in admiration or to enter and consume it wholly for myself - stars to season, crater for a spoon.

I cannot separate myself from this desire - tied to it by a phantom umbilical cord, still uncut. Women are both origin & meaning, at the heart of everything I do. I believe my reverance for the fairer sex stems from the bond I've had with my mother since birth. To my knowledge, there is nothing higher nor more pure. On afternoons when the skies are overcast, smelling of melancholy and pending rain, I can still feel her tug me from behind the navel, beckoning me to stay home when I have other plans. And suddenly I don't want to go out anymore but stay by her side, even when she hasn't said a word and is indifferent to my absence. If you could be chronically homesick for the womb, I would say that is what I am—always trying to replicate the comfort of that Holiest bed. I do this either through my relationships or my writing.

So in the same vein, I am nothing if not love. I say this not from a place of insecurity but on the contrary, as I lay here single at the time of writing and happier in myself than I've ever been. Nor do I mean I am unworthy as I stand alone; rather that women bring out the best in me. They are the reason I am a writer for one. If I am a candle, women are the wick. Without them, I would spend a lifetime living in my head, creating worlds from the memories of ghosts.

I became frustrated about expressing my depth of feeling for women around the age of eighteen; found my verbal expressions were trite and that my words held more weight on a page. To avoid sounding dramatic, I learned the art of shutting up. Now I speak about them less; orbiting instead an eternal carousel of either loving or writing about loving. Both suffice. My obsession is not Casanovian, but observant. There are lovers, yes, but there are also mothers, and teachers, and friends. As long as I have one to actively adore, either manifested or through the pen, I am content. Whether mothered or mistress, it's ambrosia & nectar all the same. The liquor between their legs is a drug; their milk soothes babies to sleep.

Writers are known to struggle with mindfulness as it can undermine craft. To write, or more specifically, to write effectively, it can be argued that one must always have one foot in the past. It is essential for us to rummage through our personal histories, then; to organise them, push down on the pulse and milk them for all they're worth. Consequently, when I am not in love, I only want to write about the world around me in an attempt to cultivate that hazy, 35mm landscape I see when infatuated. I'm restless if not constantly doing so in some way.

But when I am in love, I am brought fully, entirely into the present. I can take a break from writing and live.

As the Chinese-American poet and novelist Ha Jin so perfectly puts it:

> *My notebook has remained blank for months*
> *thanks to the light you shower*
> *around me. I have no use*
> *for my pen, which lies*
> *languorously without grief.*
>
> *Nothing is better than to live*
> *a storyless life that needs*
> *no writing for meaning -*
> *when I am gone, let others say*
> *they lost a happy man,*
> *though no one can tell how happy I was.*

So this book is for all the women I was forbidden to love but did so anyway. The women who fit themselves as windows into a world I would otherwise have spent living in on my own. Because after much time and pain, I've come to realise my favourite thing about myself is that whenever I love something I always run towards it. Every time. Even when away would be safer.

Even just to give myself a rest from the pen.

She Will Leave My Lips For Some Younger, Prettier Girl

after Clementine Von Radics

The red of her lips
should pose a stop light.
Instead they are the torero's flag
doubled, and I can't help
but charge forward.

I am all beast - bull, wolf
at full moon, and as we prowl
our illicit labyrinth of cobbled back streets
looking for a bench upon which
to unleash our appetite,
I tell her I don't understand.

Why does she want me?
I carry twice as many years
as her, but she folds them up
and hides them in the pockets
of my duffel coat. They hold me down
with a weight she offers to help me lift
and I want, I want,

I want to let her. But this sin
is my cross to bear and mine only.
Remember, I tell myself, she will abandon it
once my skin grows translucent
and the road uphill gets too tough
for her restless thighs.

But for now she is strong.
Pushes me up against the railings
with just her mouth. Mine
open in wait, hands hungrily
reaching up-skirt to grab
two halves of a peach.

She whispers *"Baby... baby"*
and instantly that's what I am.
I long to claim her as mine
but am weak; all I can muster
between moans are two words –

"My girl"

- and what does that mean?

This has to stop. I am flint
and she is the match - one stroke,
one strike too many and she could set me alight;
I will rush home to be doused
and end up setting my whole house on fire.

This needs to end. I am terrified
I will start to resent the life I have built.
I take her for lunch and ask if she wants kids;
force her to think about her future.
I take him for cocktails at all the places
on our bucket list. She takes off
the ring I bought her.
I send her a rose. Another redhead
to wet instead of me.

Each day my eyes follow her
up the stairs, darting down
as she looks my way;
head thrown back with laughs
for someone else. I mask
my loneliness behind a screen,
envy her middle finger
on the clit of the mouse.

Traffic Lights

Your colours warned of stop. Wait,

yet all I heard was go. Because once in a while you meet someone, and a small spark you've never quite acknowledged wakes up inside you and looks around - all ember-eyed and cinder-haired. She warms you right to the top with quiet awe, spreading onto your face in a sunrise grin of comprehension that this is not your first encounter but a soul reunion, and after years of slumber the universe has shifted, allowing her to poke between your ribs and ignite once more.

I wanted you from the moment you called out to me. In what capacity I did not know, but the want was there - old and smouldering. We were closest in another life; I knew from the start I was late for this one. You'd arrived decades earlier, were already sharing yourself with someone else. Arms had been ceremoniously linked, elbows tilted, champagne already trickled down the throat.

Do not be sad. I am not smiling because I am ambivalent, but because I know how this goes. And should you wish to change course now, you would glow with the light of a monster star, yes - but ultimately I would be convicted of arson. Think of the people we would burn in our trailblaze of passion. Man and boy alike would open their mouths to plead and cough up smoke. We'd rush to heat cool nights with a lover's touch only to end up charring each other with blackened fingers.

Your decision to stay with him is wise this time round. Here, your flames are far more suited to the hearth than Pudding Lane devastation. It is enough for us to share space every day. I never intended to love you into a corner.

I will see you next time, and we can try again. Because bonds like these do not break, only bend. We are eternal. Just know that for all your insecurities, your age does not phase me. In fact, quite the opposite. Your skin gleams opal from afar and the closer I look, all I see is more places I want to kiss.

Grapes & Tangerines

My nerves are alight
with you. Fibres drunk
on your seasoned body, hunger growing
the longer this orgasm you've bred
in my abdomen simmers. How long
can I be pressed close to you
without climax? I open my eyes
in the morning and am already on the edge.

Have developed a recent obsession
with grapes and tangerines, the way they burst
between my teeth to flood my mouth
with their wet. Waiting for you
is no frustration,
just delicious patience;
like living a whole life in order to transcend.

It is no secret women should be worshipped
on hands and knees, adorned
in jewels, plumped fat
with hedonism. It's time
to try on a different ring,
so slip your finger in,
hear me whimper
as you tug on me.

Cherry Pit Stomach

I am proud of my cherry pit
stomach. Have been carving
it out for some time now,
scooping up ruby flesh
in my gut grown fat
with undue emotion
the moment I sense threat
of rot; poison from yet another
woman never destined to make
a permanent home inside me.

I have been practising yoga
with my heart and its strength
is improving daily - can do crow
now; that trickster bird,
master of deceit. And I have mastered it
see, pretended not to care
for so long that now
it takes little time at all
for this to become the truth.

Last week I got over someone in a day!

Taught myself to shape-shift,
slide out of my feelings like she
did her wedding ring. Learnt
the correct way to glare
at that ink black beauty
spot on her arm, once so endearing,

until it meant nothing to me.

Just a warning she was next
to go. One more pirate
in my veins guilty of treason.

Her fiery temperament
hair
pale skin

once a delicious palette of rust on snow

now not so different
from a boy's forgotten bicycle
in winter, discarded
with the cherry stone -

just junk.

How Do You Keep a Rose
Alive Forever?

Last night, for the first time, I thought of you while in bed with someone else. I hate that people do this - trade their body for a consolation. But I am twenty five now and my quarter life crisis has led me to rely on nothing any more but my own whims. So fuck it, I made an active decision to surrender to the memory of you, closed my eyes to the image of your sunflower and daffodil yellow held against me, the flower press - your lips devouring mine, because if our time is truly up, at least this way I could spend one more moment with you. Even if it was really only with myself. And her.

Perception is everything, you see. And this is why I am content with never finding out who sent me the single red rose last week (I say this even though I have called the florist and even been into the shop to ask. We Geminis are such dual creatures.) because isn't that all we humans really have? The delicate petals of hope?

I hope it was you. Then if you never again permit yourself drunk enough to confess you think about me all the time, that perhaps there is more than one person for everyone, at least I have the most romantic gesture of all as confirmation. I change the rosewater as often as I remember, have moved my grandmother's vase to the end of my bed so that I can see it still untouched in its cellophane as I drift to sleep. And that is my only comfort. I've never looked after a plant properly, except myself. And I was doing so well with the latter, but now I've taken up menthols again because not smoking reminds me of you. The lemon cake smell of my yoga studio reminds me of you, and I practiced every day. Working towards the best version of myself brings a nostalgia for when we were dizzy with desire for one another, but we ended anyway, didn't we? So what do a few drags matter, when a pristine lifestyle and lungs could not keep you? What can I count on to bring me joy now except grabbing any fleeting pleasure by the throat and kissing it hot and thick against the wall as it passes by in a packed room? Our world can flip from the royal box; we can find true love from the gutter.

Perhaps it was symbolic that we bonded over sharing news of tragedy the year all the celebrities died. We acted more upset about the passing of people we did not know than the imminent death of us. But I'm looking for something immortal. So, even if it was not you, don't tell me. Allow me this one hope. Just place your hand friendly beneath my shoulder blades and tell me this: how do you keep a rose alive forever?

Washing Powder

You are your own brand of fragrance;
scent so good, your sweat
could be bottled and flogged
to the masses.

Smell so clean, your mother's womb
a tumble dryer,
and you tumbled out in all the whites
swaddled; extra softener.

Too Close For Comfort

Remember when coming to work was more exciting than
going home?

Now there is quiet.

Figure on my left
asking why you have not been yourself for a while.
Figure on my right
telling me our combined energy is missed.
Figure opposite
gossiping about our successors.

I have an energy people want to confide in, have found out
others here are doing what we once did. Probably with less
passion but also a lot less to lose.

I know how everyone is kissing each other and no one is coping.

Someone says your name and my heart seizes
                                    releases
                                        veins flooding
with a shock of deep red adrenaline as if I had not heard tell
of you for months
but you're sitting right next to me.

I have learnt closeness has nothing to do with proximity.

To the Grave

After everything you've done for me -
pulling strings, your effort and hard work,

I will keep my secrets like I said;
they will ride with me inside my hearse

because there are no broken hearts here but
sometimes there's something *almost* worse:

it would *crush your ego* if you knew
I had your right hand woman first.

Friday

The very nature of getting over someone
means its manifestation will never bring
the victorious release imagined
when hurting. It is a process,
not an event – we don't celebrate
what we no longer care for.

I wanted an overnight epiphany;
the sounds of shackles smacking concrete.
All I got was the gradual, dull acceptance
that now, just like everyone else,
Friday was once again
my favourite day of the week.

Two Friends

We don't *have* to speak every day
it just seems to happen that way.

Look how we've grown from complete strangers
to kin through alchemy of the blood

(although we cannot be the ones to join our families,
we make sure there's a chance for our descendants).

Sometimes we go out to eat and I barely talk.
I'm quiet when pensive or it's been a long day

but you take my silence
and raise it with your own

(I'm always worried this means
it's our last date. It never is.)

This is what it means to have love.
We conquered the honeymoon phase

of fear and blaze, recouped
after the break up that was needed

back when we didn't know what to do
with all this chemistry. Back when it reeked of hazard.

Now we are skilled apprentices in science;
have taught ourselves, each other,

to manage the flames and this is why
we can now spend days apart without a burn-

our affinity has softened
from fire into the gauze

-we know we can't be together,
so we always are.

This is as good as it gets,
but not the agonising thrum of loss,

rather something special to embrace,
a private party to enjoy.

It is the reason we order an extra morning coffee,
eat from each other's plates without asking,

why we listen before reacting
and why *friend* is the weakest word between us.

Our months together now pass by
unpinched as a quiet cloud, then in June

I'll glance back at April or May and realise
you've stripped another of my layers without my noticing.

Do you know how much of an art that is?
That I can spend my whole life stitching myself up

with spider silk, only to unravel myself to you
and rain with the least embarrassment?

It still surprises me, that night the liquor filled me up
until my eyes burst unabashedly and drenched you,

unexpecting, in my loneliest confession.
And you just held me. Even after all this.

I guess that's how I learnt you are sanctuary.
Trusted you still had me.

I knew we would walk together
how we always did, regardless of distance or weather

back through all our London landmarks
to where we needed to be.

Whether hand-in-hand
or you marching feet ahead

laughing or sulking
flirting or fighting

with you and I there is always the promise
of tomorrow. Neither of us are going anywhere.

In a room full of people you love,
it says a lot where you set your base.

I may not let you forget the time
you tried to throw me away unsuccessfully;

I know it's tiring I still make you pay for it.
But no matter how many times my young heart parades

its new marvels in front of you
like your row of ten tequilas,

it is still you I search for when the lights
come on and everyone calls their taxis.

It is you who takes me home,
the one who rocks me to sleep.

Jade

The irony

To open my heart chakra
I am told to think of the colour
green. But all I've been doing
is thinking of green -
the colour of your name,
my name, us.

Still when you encourage
me to open up to you,
the shutters of my chest
roll down and my guards rise.
All the while your name
gets prettier every time
I hear it, see it,
think it.

Not a fan of the colour,
I took mine with apathy
but yours - the same
number of letters and syllables,
sparkles.

We'd go well together
in the home, I think.
Pantone agree.

The irony

Each time I do reveal myself
to you it proves worth it.
I guess it is not you I am wary
of darling, but my past
repeating itself. I know
if I use bricks from old pain

I will build the same house,
just give me a little more time,
a little more reason to trust you.
Because sometimes my past
washes over me like a flood

and to be defensive
is my only defense.

Unteach me this relishing of loneliness,
this thriving off isolation.
For on those rare occasions
our souls *do* speak
the sun breaks through the clouds;
I want to say hello to strangers on the street.

Scales
after Phoebe Stuckes

You love everything
and everyone
is what they'd say
about us but we didn't
love that.

Scrunched up our disco noses
knowing the contrary.
Let them think we're too nice
we'd sigh, *too sweet,*
like dessert double stuffed
or everything belonging
to the second bear.

We were happy, that's all.
Not averse to aversion
when it was called for.
Piss me off, and I'll fuck you over
you laughed in mock retort
to an audience of no one
but me

then we kissed
as I lit you a cigarette
round the back and hanging
from my lips it crackled and spat,
as we listed all the ways
we could hate, if necessary.

They'd see
we agreed, but we only showed
ourselves because look at us now,
look! How we *don't even look*
at each other.

The vindictive streak
we were so pleased to curate
ended up smeared like bullshit
across our very own work of art.

We didn't end on the worst terms
(too nice for that, obviously)
but still, we ended
because you broke promises.
Both important ones to him,
made in front of God
and those to me, that you
don't even remember making.

But hey, at least you kept
to one! I did piss you off
and you did fuck me over,
and now I can tell you loathe me
from the blocking and subliminal posts;
and the way you didn't even text me
on my birthday which is
between the bull and the crab,
yet it wasn't me who couldn't choose
between charging head on
and scuttling away when it was time
to fight for us -

it was you in the middle
of the angel and the scorpion,
which is to say you are a Libra,
with two arms that can't bare to carry
more of one thing than another
and when I got too heavy
you dropped me.

So hate is a strong word
but still I use it here
provisionally, on the condition
you do nothing to fix our fracture.

And you won't. For I know you
despite yourself, how you sit
on those scales, small
and quiet between beam
and fulcrum, waiting
for the ache of missing me to fade
because it's easier than addressing
what's wrong.

So carry on like nothing happened,
but if you ever see me again
please don't act like you know me.

You don't.

You might have touched
me once, but I burnt you
with the last new moon
and I have not felt you since.
Your palms carry no weight,
remember.

I really hope I never do,
you know - see you again.
Have lost the energy
to be polite.

I wonder - would we
have found it funny that day,
had we the foresight,
that we don't love everyone at all,
fuck, we couldn't even
love each other

and look what we destroyed
by proving ourselves right.

Forgetting

the more I think about you
the less I remember
your name hovers
with the memory
that thing of us
around me
cloud pulled through
a ticker tape timer
but it's punching out your freckles
one by one
with every tock
the leaking rains
smudging your mouth
softening the bounce
at the tip of your nose

I know these exist
because I attached importance to them
but now when I come close
in my head
your face almost
almost
could be anyone's

I Can't Hear You

when you claim
to be the injured party.
Can't pour
from an empty cup
to fill you up
when it's you
who drank
and drained mine.
I won't listen
to you make excuses
from the heartbreak of your past
when you have no plans
to keep me in your future.
When entrusted
with a heart I'll pump it
swoll with understanding,
am all ears for those
who never offer more
than they can give.
But don't expect me
to feel bad for you
when you've enticed me
with a red thread
and no ankle to tie it round.
I know you've had it the hardest-
really I do,
but I can't listen to your pain
until you ensure me you
won't add to mine.
That's just how it goes.
I've forced myself deaf.
All my life I've been patient
and now I am tired.
Have given for far too long
without being cherished in return.

So I'm sorry but I can't be
sorry any more, can't see
past your tears if not one
is for me when mine
are only for you.

Tough Love

I've become an expert at accepting rejection,
knowing the effect it can have if I resist;
harbouring in my cells
then solidifying:
a grudge.

Now I just "Okay" the end,
inhale into the impact
of iron doors slamming shut
around my heart again: one more
layer of armour. Act like nothing
happened so my opponent cannot tell
if I ever, in fact, gave a fuck.

I always joked you were my
commanding officer and I,
your mini-me mould,
but I did not think for a moment
that this
is how
you would toughen me up.

Noli Me Tangere (For Caesar's I Am)

You can't concentrate but you have to. Exams are soon and the Roman love myths are all relevant; the doe in Wyatt's translation of *Whoso List to Hunt* reminds you of her. Her, with the diamond necklace; all teasing and tripping. How gleefully she flees from you. You should remember this time last year when you felt the same about another girl, how at times it paralysed you beyond motivation. You should reflect on how the tables have turned and your lack of feeling for her now. This is surely encouragement enough. But you haven't taken the medicine of her voice for hours; your aching muscles have relaxed like your puppeteer has put you down, and there is something self-destructively comforting in just lying there and letting the waves of love wash over you like Dido, wounded. Even when you probably aren't.

Black & Blue

This poem is not written
after the fact, like my others.
It is not written in peace. I force
myself through these lines
with the gash across my insides
still fresh as the one your legs
clench to conceal, for it is here
my heart has dropped and leaks.

It is not always agony,
sometimes it's just pain.
And these veins just plums,
battered and strung out.

Sex is not enough
to save us anymore.
I'd have to consume
all he did not reach.
Suck the wet salt of regret
from your eyelashes, turn you
inside out and write my name
in tongues all over every inch, shift
                                        your
                                     hips
onto my face and cup my mouth
around your cunt to drink
your golden; take the worst
from you so he no longer
wears that medal of brass.

How will I ever forgive you?

When every time I enter
I'm reminded how he tunnelled
through my passage, wider now
so that I cannot feel the take

and give of the entrance
to the bed you wanted for my child.
That you could beckon
a stranger to you in the dark,
ignorant of his face - mine too,
and let him undo all my care.

I have not felt resentment like this for years.
Vow never to again.

A Mother's Sacrifice

If your mother is sad
and you have shreds of orange
sunshine glittering in you,
give them back to her.

Wake her up with them
as the dusty beam of morning
yawns through her window,
sprawls across her Sunday sheets.
Drizzle them, golden-glossed
over breakfast pancakes
like the finest Manuka
and if she likes it with pulp,
squeeze them into her juice,
flecks of serotonin grated
on the jelly on her marmalade.
Wipe them, tender on the tanning mitt
down the valley of her spine.
Leave some in a kiss placed soft
between her shoulders to signify
you are done. She is bronzed.

In the evening, pop them in tealights
around her home, a votive
for every year she kept you afloat.
Remember - she made them
after all, they were hers before
she put them in you.

Emma

I disagree with Shakespeare's
Juliet. There is so much in a name.
How could there not be
when yours means *whole*
or universal?

Emma. Heart of perfect
symmetry, inspiring harmony
between body and mind;
ether and earth. Hold a mirror
to its centre and the reflection
is immaculate. You only need to look
around the room to see it, all
your students echoed
before you on an alpine horizon,
painted on the back wall of our
yoga studio.

As above,
so below.

When life moves
fast you are permission to pause;
to harness energy and sit with
it awhile. And as you tread
amongst us I delight
in all I've manifested. Even this,
here in our crypt - candle in hand
to light your path along
the labyrinth of our bodies held
in Sphinx. What more could I ask?
I've your voice in the dark,
reminder we are timeless.

Em - soft hum,
the pause between thought and speech,
offered - for example - when you
confuse your left & right
or that time I asked you to describe
your experience with sun-gazing
and you couldn't. You tried,
running strong fingers through honey
hair, earl grey gaze trailing off into the distance
but faltered, blinded by the memory
and unable to find the right words.
I wanted to call out to you then
that I too understood,
in your presence, the incapacity
to articulate a feeling
so profound.

Mm - deep core,
balancing beginning and end
the way Wednesday
does my week. Gentle sigh
a dove released seeing your face
after a long day; balm to my 9-5
ache.

Ma – open finish,
the space you allow
when suggesting,
vowel not closed unto
itself but receptive to the sounds
which succeed it. What I am saying
is it's no coincidence
babies choose this as their first word,
so pure they repeat it
once deciding it is time
to allocate a sound to love. So yes

you by any other name would smell as sweet
but not feel the same in the mouth.
Names are heavy things, weighted

with years by the nuance
in which they have been called,
colouring a lens
through which one is identified. And yours,
I imagine only uttered gently
through the lips of one
who loves you, or with tender concern
which in itself, I think, says
everything about you. So this is why

names are important.
Because I have said
too much. When *Emma*
is enough.

Stream of Consciousness of a Young Soul upon Finding Her Old Soulmate

What is it like to still wear your nimbus? Is it time-consuming to weave between your golden plaits each morning and that's why most days you wear your hair long, like nectar dripping down your back? *(That back! In motion! Churned by the dolphins of your shoulder blades into caramelised sugar glass!)* Is that why? I know you're tired. I feel it in you because I knew you before - eons ago, plus your car is a mess and you're often flustered. That's the price sometimes, isn't it? Of following your dreams. I know it too. But what's it like to show up for everyone else's each day regardless? To be tonic after a long day? The best thing since sliced bread? (Yesterday, I Googled the year sliced bread was invented, to check it isn't the best thing since you. Don't be offended. You're just *so much older* than me in this world. I wanted to be certain). And who is nourishing *you* now? You beam and glow like you did in the last place, so someone must be doing it. Then again, you're probably solar-powered now aren't you? Self-sufficient. Still, wouldn't it be nice for someone else to light you *for* you? I've learned your smell here - what is it, doves? Do you remember me? From our soul cloud? We're from the same one, you know. I see you visit sometimes, in those rare moments someone else carries the conversation and your energy is not demanded. How is it there, back home? I call it home because something in me recognises your face, and it isn't my eyes. That face has been everywhere with me before, on centuries of deathbeds and in all the liminal spaces. Witnessing it again has meant I've had to ration our eye contact. It's too indulgent, makes me feel I'm wearing my heart on the outside of my body. I know you've known me before and I'm scared that if you look too long you'll realise too. I don't think you're ready to remember just yet. But give us a few more months like this and the secret will be out. This makes me nervous. And that is why I love the way you blink. The dramatic kiss of your eyelids has such intention. An illustration of confusion! These temporary blips in your calm afford me a moment to recollect myself and break the connection, for you look like you've been spun out of orbit, and this unglitches the matrix. How did you keep your power to manipulate time? A second is still a lifetime with you. I have so much I want to tell you from the years you've missed and talk quickly, you might have noticed. But you never close me off. Are so polite, so gentle; neither disputing my convictions nor agreeing with them the way one would expect a soulmate would. You neither sugar coat for me nor deny but leave me open to interpretation. Instruct me to find my own answers without giving them to me, to set my drishti to within, to remember I am timeless. These are the moments I feel you've got it all figured out. Then I cannot resist to look at you for confirmation and lose my balance like a drunken sailor. It is not time yet. Sometimes, we notice rare moments in life where everything is exactly how we'd dream it from a bird's eye view or a film. This is how I feel when you guide me. And sometimes, when I slow, I manage to catch what I am manifesting in the moment I'm creating it without rushing onto the next errand as people on this earth are quick to do. It's always in these moments that you are in the room. And what did you mean? What did you mean when I wrote you that poem and gave it to you, and you turned away from me, confessing your tears only to ceiling before recollecting yourself and announcing "You were sent to me." Does that mean you do remember? Have you been hiding too, the fact you've known all along? Because I found you again, right when my body wanted to die. On this planet, they say the greatest teacher will send you back to yourself. On this planet, they also say, *When the student is ready, the teacher appears. When the student is truly ready, the teacher disappears.* I hope I am never truly ready then. You gifted my body back to me and now I want to offer it to you. Not as a sacrifice, not at any lack to myself - but with my sweat as a libation. Tell me, will that nourish you?

Quest For the Right Shade of Blue

To me, you are Blue. (Not the mood, but the hue.) Have kindled a colour known for its chill; distilled a word so often stained in sadness with fresh meaning. I can't be sure if it's the clothes you wear or your aura that first decided this for me; only that since meeting you I suddenly recall Blue's subtle ghost in so many of my favourite things. The pale milk and petals of the heroine's bath in a TV film that moved me as a teenager. Clementine's hair. Electric Light Orchestra's best song. Viagra flavoured ice cream with my ex in Rome. More recently, decadent sponge of Queen Anne's cake in The Favourite. The way an older woman's veins wrap around her forearms like thick rope. Your overalls. My bedsheets when I first met you.

Have my eyes just now opened?

Both voted most loved, yet never ostentatious, I've been trying to find the right shade to encapsulate you but fall short. No chart is consistent.

Pantone: too broad
Crayola: too limited

and the rest too exhaustive to list. Like Sky (a shade I *almost* settled on) I guess you're an expanse that can't be boxed by Dulux. Still, I've employed helpers. Turned into Veruca Salt's father about this, got friends who know you helping me decide exactly which blue you are. Have them plunging wrist-deep into all manner of lazuli cavities searching for the Sapphire ticket with your name on. I hosted a dinner party - whale heart as the main to gorge on, midnight flavoured jelly flecked with stars for dessert. Found the guests covered in zebra-finch feathers (have you *seen* their forget-me-not wings?) - an avian pillow fight by the time taxis arrived.

Even then I was not satisfied. Steve from work phoned me at my desk last week and asked, hurriedly. "Are you busy? Run outside a moment and look up. I've found the colour of your friend!" This is what I mean when I call it Quest. That even our security guard knows. And he has come closest yet: Dusk. (Give the man a pay rise.)

I have spent nights Googling swatches until blue in the face and that is when I realised the more I check, the more there are to check and anyway, perhaps the only ones worth searching are your denim eyes, how they move along the spectrum depending how you feel that day; a pair of mood ring irises.

For when we found each other, I was depressed. Dragged myself from my Spring bed in search of a mentor to sign the paper promising me a new future. It didn't have to be you but you were there. You signed it. It's like I'd been blue for so long I manifested its personification that day - a diamond I did not expect. And you taught me, among other things, that I did not have to be happy to love. Instead you met me where I was, showing the beauty in every colour. Assuring me just by existing that I did not have to rush the rainbow climb, but could be guided through it from the shades of its bottom rungs with presence and enjoy the view

of entire sky and sea (you are).
As above, so below.

So be it Dusk, Indigo, Periwinkle,
all I know is when I think of Blue
I don't think of cold any more.

Acknowledgements

Emma Croft,
who drenched my life in light again.

Christina Flourentzou,
for the closing of this book;
the resting of my pen.

No more shutting up.

LAY OUT YOUR UNREST